ABOVE MACKINAC

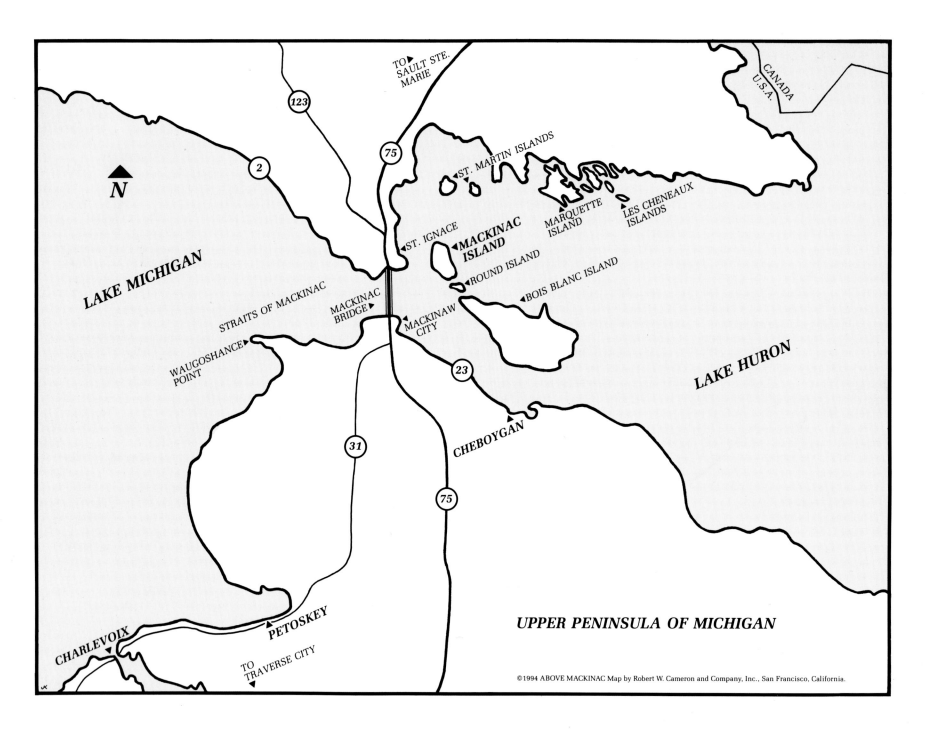

TO ► SAULT STE. MARIE

CANADA
U.S.A.

123

75

2

N

ST. MARTIN ISLANDS

► ST. MARTIN ISLANDS

LAKE MICHIGAN

MARQUETTE ISLAND

LES CHENEAUX ISLANDS

► ST. IGNACE

◄ **MACKINAC ISLAND**

► ROUND ISLAND

► BOIS BLANC ISLAND

STRAITS OF MACKINAC

MACKINAC BRIDGE ►

◄ MACKINAW CITY

WAUGOSHANCE POINT ►

23

LAKE HURON

31

CHEBOYGAN ►

75

PETOSKEY ►

UPPER PENINSULA OF MICHIGAN

CHARLEVOIX ▼

TO ▼ TRAVERSE CITY

©1994 ABOVE MACKINAC Map by Robert W. Cameron and Company, Inc., San Francisco, California.

(Opposite) The Straits of Mackinac is the crossroads of the upper Great Lakes where the crystal blue waters of Lake Huron and Lake Michigan flow together beneath the mighty Mackinac Bridge.

The century-old Grand Hotel is the most dramatic
example of Mackinac Island's rich architectural heritage.

(Opposite) Uninhabited Round Island *(foreground)* provides a peaceful contrast to world-
famous Mackinac Island which attracts nearly one million visitors every summer.

Only eight miles in circumference, Mackinac Island is filled with great natural beauty, unparalleled history and every imaginable flavor of fudge!

(Opposite) Every summer the narrow channel between Mackinac Island *(left)* and Round Island is a busy thoroughfare for commercial freighters, ferry boats and pleasure craft.

Dominated by the stone walls of Fort Mackinac and lined with quaint, white clapboard houses, Mackinac Island's harbor is among the most picturesque in America.

(Opposite) The Round Island Lighthouse has been a steadfast sentinel greeting visitors to nearby Mackinac Island since 1895.

Putting together a book like Above Mackinac can be enormously complex and requires the help of many friendly, even dedicated people. So, for their encouragement and expertise, I thank the following:

David Armour, Robert Burger, Robert Ekstrand, John Goy, Linda Henry, Tina Hodge, Jane Manoogian, Richard Manoogian, Mimi Musser, Carl Nold, Patricia O'Grady, William Porter, Lorone Porter, Robert Raisch and Susie Raisch.

Special thanks to Barry BeDour for expert piloting and consultation.

For assistance in researching the historical aerial photography, acknowledgement is made to Mackinac State Historic Parks for pages 20, 22, 24.
and
The National Aeronautics and Space Administration for pages 60 and 70.

CAMERON and COMPANY

543 Howard Street   San Francisco, California 94105 USA   415/777-5582

Library of Congress Catalog Number: 94-094165
ABOVE MACKINAC ISBN: 0-918684-38-2
©1994 by Robert W. Cameron and Company, Inc. All rights reserved.

First Printing, 1994

Book design by
JANE OLAUG KRISTIANSEN

Color processing by The New Lab, San Francisco   Cameras by Pentax
Typography by What A Beautiful Setting and Minnowillo, San Francisco
Retouching by Jerome Vloeberghs and Alicemarie Mutrux
Color Separations and Printing in South Korea

ABOVE MACKINAC

AND
SOME OF ITS NEIGHBORS

by ROBERT CAMERON

A new collection of historical and
original aerial photographs

with text by
PHIL PORTER

For David Eriksson
Phil Porter
July 1994

CAMERON and COMPANY, San Francisco, California

INTRODUCTION

Mackinac Island has been my summer home since childhood and a part of my family for generations. Growing up on the island my summer days were filled with unique experiences – exploring ancient sea caves, playing golf on a War of 1812 battlefield and galloping horses (after I mucked out their stalls!) on cliff-side bridle paths. While in college and graduate school I worked as a tour guide at historic Fort Mackinac and upon graduation I became a full-time historian and curator for Mackinac State Historic Parks. After twenty years of research and interpretation, Mackinac's rich and varied history still fascinates me.

The Straits of Mackinac appeared over fifteen thousand years ago as the glaciers of the last ice age withdrew to the north. Mile-high floes of ice scoured deep ravines into the earth's surface and filled them with melting waters – the Great Lakes were formed. At the center of the upper Great Lakes the Straits of Mackinac, with its spectacular islands and deep, cool waters, emerged to connect lakes Michigan and Huron and separate Michigan's two peninsulas. The earliest settlers migrated from the south and these waters became busy highways during the warm summers and abandoned, frozen wastelands in winter – a pattern that continues at the Straits today.

For centuries, Native Americans paddled fragile birch bark canoes to the Straits every summer in search of whitefish and lake trout. So plentiful was their catch, that they called these waters "the home of the fish." The native people were particularly attracted to the hump-backed island with curious rock formations that they called "Michilimackinac" or Land of the Great Turtle. Today Ojibway and Odawa people still revere Mackinac Island as a sacred place of great spiritual importance.

Drawn by the Native settlements, French missionaries and fur traders came to the Straits of Mackinac in the 1670s. Jesuit Priest Jacques Marquette established the mission of St. Ignatius Loyola on Mackinac Island in 1670 and moved it to the north side of the Straits (today St. Ignace) the following year. French fur traders also established their headquarters at St. Ignace which soon became a strategic summer depot connecting the rich fur lands south, west and north of Mackinac with the commercial markets of the east coast and Europe. To protect the lucrative fur trade, the French constructed Fort de Buade at St. Ignace in 1690. For the next 250 years fur traders, with the help of the military, continued to use the Straits of Mackinac as the central supply station and transshipment point of upper Great Lakes fur trade.

In 1715 French missionaries, soldiers and traders moved to the south side of the Straits where they constructed Fort Michilimackinac (today Mackinaw City). At first a simple and quiet outpost, Fort Michilimackinac flourished as a prosperous trading village after British authorities took control in the 1760s. A nearby village of more than one hundred houses – known as the "suburbs" – developed when the fort walls could no longer hold the expanding population.

The American Revolution had a lasting impact on the Straits of Mackinac. Fearful of a possible American gunboat attack, British commander Patrick Sinclair moved his garrison from the mainland to the protective bluffs of nearby Mackinac Island in 1781. The "suburban" civilians and fur traders followed the soldiers and established the village of Mackinac Island below the fort and around the island's natural harbor. British soldiers were still hewing logs and splitting shingles for the new fort when they learned of the American victory at Yorktown. Two years later the Treaty of Paris deeded the Straits of Mackinac to the young United States. American troops did not occupy the fort until 1796 and promptly lost it to the British at the outbreak of the War of 1812. But the treaty ending that war again granted the Straits area to the United States and

American troops returned to Fort Mackinac in 1815.

John Jacob Astor's American Fur Company flourished on Mackinac Island following the War of 1812. In the 1820s, millions of dollars worth of furs flowed through the company's buildings on Market Street before they were shipped to eastern markets. Mackinac furs made Astor America's first millionaire. By the early 1830s the trade declined as the region's fur-bearing animals were trapped out and European styles changed. Islanders turned to fishing to support their families and Mackinac Island became an important upper Great Lakes fish processing and shipping center.

After the Civil War trading and fishing gave way to tourism as the main economy of the Straits of Mackinac. Mackinac Island, with its delightful combination of natural beauty, historic charm and healthy environment, became a summer destination for travelers from throughout the country. In response to the island's growing popularity, the federal government established Mackinac National Park in 1875 and Fort Mackinac's commandant became the park superintendent. This was the country's second national park, created only three years after Yellowstone Park in Wyoming Territory. Steamboats and railroads extended their service to the Straits of Mackinac and transported thousands of tourists north each summer. Soon the face of Mackinac began to change as local entrepreneurs remodeled old fur warehouses and fish shanties into resort hotels, curio shops and confectionery stores.

The swell of visitors in the 1880s crowded the dusty streets and overwhelmed the island's modest hotels. Construction of the magnificent Grand Hotel in 1887 resolved the room crunch and forever changed the character of Mackinac Island. The elegant hotel attracted prominent socialites from Detroit and Chicago who transformed Mackinac into a Midwestern Newport. Mackinac Island was the most fashionable summer place in the upper Great Lakes and visitors of great wealth were eager to be seen promenading along the Grand Hotel's classical, columned porch. Not all summer visitors were content staying in a hotel, even one as luxurious as the Grand. Those who wanted more permanent roots built opulent summer homes along the cedar-lined bluffs overlooking the Straits of Mackinac.

Mackinac Island was a flourishing resort when the federal government decided to remove the soldiers from the fort and transfer the national park to Michigan in 1895. The fort and public lands became Michigan's first state park and, in many ways, the island hasn't changed much since then. The preservation programs of the Mackinac State Historic Parks and the 1896 ban on automobiles are responsible for the island's unique turn-of-the-century character.

Although Mackinac Island is the focal point, it shares this rich history with many of its neighboring islands and towns. From Cheboygan on the east to Waugoshance Point on the west, the Straits of Mackinac has a long and fascinating history. Like Mackinac Island, the northwestern Michigan cities of Harbor Springs, Petoskey, Charlevoix and Traverse City, have been popular summer resorts for more than a century. To the north, Sault Ste. Marie is Michigan's oldest city, and one that has been inextricably linked to Mackinac since the earliest days of fur trade and missionary activity.

Bob Cameron's aerial photographs have reinvigorated my sense of wonder and excitement about the Mackinac region of northern Michigan. From his lofty vantage point Mr. Cameron has beautifully captured the natural beauty and awe-inspiring combination of lake, land and sky in this place we call Mackinac.

— Phil Porter

Today restored Fort Mackinac is the oldest original military site in the Midwest and a jewel in the Michigan state parks system. Fourteen original military buildings are filled with informative displays, exciting audio-visual programs and interactive exhibits for children. The fort's Tea Room offers light lunches and a panoramic view of the Straits of Mackinac from the officers' stone quarters veranda.

(Opposite) Fort Mackinac has a rich history; built during the American Revolution, site of the first battle of the War of 1812, a strategic outpost in the upper Great Lakes and, finally, a historic curiosity for Victorian tourists.

The city of Mackinac Island is nestled below the fort and around the bay. The lakeside village reflects its original 18th-century configuration. Water Street (today known as Huron Street) hugs the bay and provides access to the boat docks. Market Street, connected by narrow lanes that have not been widened to accommodate modern vehicles, is one block north.

(*Opposite*) The historic character of Mackinac Island is preserved by the ban on automobiles and extensive use of horses and carriages. The auto ban dates back to the summer of 1896 when a young dandy brought his noisy horseless carriage to the island's quaint, dusty streets. When the local horses, busy pulling sightseeing carriages, met their first car pandemonium ensued. The frightened tour drivers quickly petitioned the city council which issued a prohibition against the noisome monstrosities.

Mackinac Island is known for its ancient and beautiful lilac trees. Marquette Park below Fort Mackinac displays a wonderful variety of lilacs from brilliant white to deep purple. Islanders celebrate with an annual lilac festival when the trees bloom in mid-June.

(Opposite) As many as 15,000 tourists visit Mackinac Island on a busy summer day. As they dodge the bikes and buggies on busy Main Street, visitors are treated to a unique combination of sounds including boat whistles, sea gull cries and cannon blasts from the fort.

Life on Mackinac Island has always revolved around its crescent-shaped harbor where boats have safely moored since the days of the American Revolution. New docks were constructed and others enlarged as the island's popularity increased between 1946 (*above*) and today.

One major difference between the Mackinac Island harbor of the 1940s (*above*) and today is the absence of large passenger steamboats. Once a stylish and elegant way to come to the island, these luxurious liners became obsolete when modern highways provided greater automobile access to northern Michigan in the late 1950s.

Every summer since 1898 Mackinac Island has been the finish line for the world-famous, 330-mile Chicago to Mackinac sailboat race. Lake Huron sailors initiated the 235-mile Port Huron to Mackinac race in 1928. The island's yacht dock has expanded considerably since the 1950s (*above*) to accommodate the nearly 250 sailboats that participate in the races today.

The view from the Mackinac Bridge *(left)* is spectacular. Miles of crystal clear blue waters, picturesque islands, stately iron ore freighters and rooster-tailed ferry boats *(below)* fill the Straits area horizon.

(Opposite) Mackinac sailors stretch brightly colored spinnaker sails on the harborside grass to dry in the warm Mackinac sun following the races.

The south end of Mackinac Island with St. Ignace and St. Helena Island in the distance.

(Opposite) By the late 1880s the small village could no longer handle the surge of summer visitors and the builders of the now-famous Grand Hotel (left) choose a bluff north of the village as the site for their ambitious project. A nearby cow pasture became the Grand Hotel's golf course after the turn of the century.

28

Grand Hotel's large serpentine-shaped swimming pool on the lower terrace was used for several Esther Williams' swimming scenes in the 1946 film "This Time For Keeps." Thirty-three years later Hollywood returned to Mackinac and featured Grand Hotel in "Somewhere in Time."

The hotel was built by Harbor Springs contractor Charles Caskey, known as a quick and competent builder. Caskey confirmed his hard-earned reputation by using a three-hundred man crew to construct the Grand in less than four mounths in the spring of 1887!

(Opposite) The incomparable Grand Hotel, Mackinac Island's best-known landmark, was built in 1887 by three transportation companies whose boats and trains brought hordes of Victorian summer visitors to the island. An immediate success, the stately Grand Hotel transformed Mackinac Island into the Midwest's most fashionable summer watering place.

The Tea Garden below the hotel is the site of festive occasions
including evening barbecues and the Labor Day Jazz Festival.

The island's most elegant cottages hold forth at the top of the West Bluff. These picturesque wooden castles boldly proclaim Victorian elegance with sweeping verandas, rising towers, protruding bays and receding porches. Built in the 1880s and '90s for $5,000 or less, these opulent mansions are now worth more than $1,000,000!

(Opposite) Mackinac Island has its own definition of summer cottage. Hardly the rustic cabins that the term "cottage" suggests, the island's summer homes are some of the finest examples of Victorian architecture in the Midwest.

Like Grand Hotel, most of the summer cottages close in the winter. The water pipes are drained, the windows shuttered and the owners go away — usually south — leaving these cavernous old homes to fend for themselves during the long Mackinac winters.

(Opposite) Just beyond the West Bluff is Hubbard's Annex. Once an 80-acre farm, Chicago businessman Gurdon S. Hubbard transformed these rocky fields into the Island's first summer cottage community in 1882.

In 1901 Lawrence Young of Chicago built this magnificent cottage for $15,000 on a wooded bluff west of Fort Mackinac. In 1945 the state of Michigan purchased the home for $15,000 for use as the executive summer residence of Michigan's governor. The Governor's Residence commands a wide-angle view of the Straits of Mackinac from above Grand Hotel's Jewel Golf Course.

(Opposite) Cottages on the Island's East Bluff nestle back into the cedars along the road between Fort Mackinac (far left) and Arch Rock. For more than a century, East Bluff cottagers have enjoyed spectacular views of the town and harbor in front, with miles of wooded roads and bridle paths behind.

Mackinac Island's largest summer cottage is Stonecliffe, built by wealthy Chicago meatpacker Michael Cudahy in 1904. The Tudor Revival cottage was refitted as a summer hotel in 1971.

(Opposite) The original two hundred acre Stonecliffe estate has been subdivided to include red-roofed condominiums adjacent to the mansion, the Woodbluff cottage community and Woods Golf Course along the bluff beyond the airport.

Below the East Bluff, Mission Point Resort dominates the east end of the island. Most of the resort's buildings were built by Moral Re-Armament which established its headquarters on Mackinac Island in the early 1940s. The group constructed Mackinac College on Mission Point in the 1960s. Although the college lasted only four years, the classrooms and dormitories have been transformed into one of the island's largest resorts.

Mackinac Island State Park encompasses more than eighty percent of the island. Established as Michigan's first state park in 1895, this unique preserve contains a wonderful variety of natural and historic resources including Wawashkamo Golf Course. Laid out in 1899, Wawashkamo is Michigan's oldest nine-hole golf course still in use.

Point aux Pins, on the north end of the island, is far from the noise and congestion of downtown. In the fall this quiet forest of oak, maple and evergreen trees comes alive with color.

In 1812 British soldiers constructed Fort George on Mackinac Island's highest ridge. Renamed Fort Holmes by American troops in 1815, the small fort fell into disuse and its ruins were replaced by an observation tower in 1856. A replica of the old fort was constructed as a W.P.A. project in the 1930s.

Mackinac Island's impressive limestone formations have captured the imagination of visitors for centuries. Sugar Loaf is the island's largest limestone stack, reaching 75 feet above the forest floor.

(Opposite) Arch Rock has buttressed the island's east shore for more than 4,000 years. Depending on which story you fancy, Arch Rock was formed either by the tears of an Indian maiden separated from her lover, or by ancient lake erosion.

Harrisonville *(center)* is one of the island's small, year-round neighborhoods. Down from a population of 3,000 in the summer (plus the nearly one million visitors!), only 600 residents live on the Island all year.

(Opposite) North of Grand Hotel are the barns and corrals of Mackinac Island Carriage Tours, Inc., the world's largest horse-drawn tour company. Carriage Tours uses more than 300 buggy-toting horses for unique sightseeing tours of the island. The horses were all on the road when this photograph was taken!

Mackinac Island, with Round Island and Bois Blanc Island in the distance. Mackinac Island has one of northern Michigan's busiest airports during the summer. But in winter the island airport is the only conduit to the mainland after the ferry boats stop and before snowmobiles can cross on the ice.

(Opposite) Passenger ferry boats have traversed the waters between Mackinac Island and the mainland since the 1870s. For visitors, the ferry boat ride is a part of the "Mackinac" experience. For residents and commuters it is a part of transportation life on "the rock."

The ferry ride to the island from St. Ignace and Mackinaw City is a feast for the senses: Panoramic views of the "Mighty Mac" Bridge, the sounds of buoy bells, freighter whistles and squawking seagulls, and the bracing scent of northern Michigan air as it blows out of pine forests over the fresh, cool waters.

(Opposite) The south end of Mackinac with Round Island, Bois Blanc Island and Cheboygan in the distance.

The Straits of Mackinac is a busy water highway, especially for the summer ferry boats that serve Mackinac Island. In winter ice breakers stationed in Cheboygan and St. Ignace cut channels through the frozen Straits allowing freighters to bring heating oil and gasoline to northern Michigan.

(Opposite) The Straits of Mackinac is a feast for the eyes; shimmering blue waters, evergreen islands and dazzling orange sunsets.

Mackinaw City is the northernmost point of Michigan's lower peninsula. Centuries before Europeans settled here, Native Americans established summer fishing villages on this point which they called Pe-quod-e-nonge, "the headland." In the foreground Wawatam Beach is lined with turn-of-the-century summer cottages, and in the distance Chippewa Bay (*also shown opposite*) provides safe mooring for private yachts and Mackinac Island ferry boats.

Old Mackinaw Point lighthouse first beamed its guiding light to passing ships in 1892. The light tower is a formidable bastion rising above the castle-like lightkeeper's residence. Like so many nineteenth-century Great Lakes lighthouses, Old Mackinaw Point was replaced by unromantic but thoroughly efficient light buoys in 1957.

(Opposite) Mackinaw City is home to Fort Michilimackinac (1715-1781), a strategic military post and the central depot of the upper Great Lakes fur trade in the eighteenth century. Today Colonial Michilimackinac has been rediscovered through the research and archaeology programs of Mackinac State Historic Parks. Exciting interpretive programs, dramatic reenactments and on-going archaeological excavations bring to life the reconstructed village.

This infrared U2 photo (in which green shows red) was taken from 65,000 feet. It shows the Mackinac Bridge connecting the upper and lower Peninsulas.

St. Ignace is on the north side of the Straits, connected to Mackinaw City and Michigan's lower peninsula by the Mackinac Bridge. Like the rest of the region, St. Ignace is a quiet village in the winter and a booming tourist town in the summer, especially during a hugely popular antique auto show weekend. Moran Bay in St. Ignace provides safe haven for ferry boats, fishing tugs and pleasure craft. More than three centuries ago French voyageurs in fur-laden birch bark canoes sought refuge here.

Historic Mill Creek is a unique northern Michigan park that celebrates the early industrial history and natural beauty of the Straits of Mackinac. The original water-powered sawmill produced thousands of planks, beams and boards used to construct buildings on Mackinac Island in the early nineteenth century. Mackinac State Historic Parks has reconstructed the sawmill and created miles of interpretive trails featuring active beaver dams.

(Opposite) Bois Blanc is the largest island in the Straits of Mackinac and a deer hunter's paradise. Most hunters journey to the island by car ferry from Cheboygan, but adventurous Mackinac Islanders scoot across the frigid, November waters in small outboards to search for Bois Blanc whitetails.

Cedarville Bay and the adjacent channels are well protected by the Les Cheneaux Islands, making it an ideal recreation area for boaters and fishermen. The sheltered bays and quiet coves provide some of the finest perch, pike, bass, brown trout and herring fishing in the region.

(Opposite) The village of Cedarville, nestled along the northeast shore of the Straits of Mackinac, is a mainland port and launching site for residents of the nearby Les Cheneaux Islands.

The Les Cheneaux Islands as seen from Lake Huron with Cedarville in the distance. This intricate chain of 36 islands was carved from the earth's surface by a massive glacier more than 12,000 years ago.

(Opposite) Marquette Island is the largest of the Les Cheneaux Islands. The island's Les Cheneaux Club *(lower right)* is home to many late nineteenth-century summer homes that rival Mackinac Island's magnificent cottages.

Hessel is the western port city of the Les Cheneaux Islands. Mertaugh Boat Works *(center right)* became the world's first Chris Craft Boat dealership in 1926. Appropriately, Hessel is the site of an annual antique boat show which displays some of the finest wooden motor and sail boats on the Great Lakes.

(Opposite) The picturesque Les Cheneaux Islands, separated by narrow channels and curving bays, are a study in island variety. Tiny Dollar Island *(center)* is home to a single cottage, while Marquette Island *(behind)* has 36 miles of coastline and hundreds of acres of forests supporting a wide variety of wildlife.

Another U2 photo pinpoints Waugoshance Point where the
currents are the most treacherous in the Great Lakes.

(Opposite) The rocky archipelago of Waugoshance Point marks the western entrance to the
Straits of Mackinac. Waugoshance, Ojibway for "little fox," is home to fragile plants and grasses
as well as nesting sea birds and waterfowl. This fragile ecosystem is a protected natural area
within Wilderness State Park.

Waugoshance Light *(left)* was constructed in 1856 to guide wooden-hulled schooners and side-wheeling steamships around hazardous rocky shallows that lurk beneath the western portal of the Straits. Replaced by White Shoal Light *(opposite page, top photo)* in 1910, Waugoshance was used as a practice bombing target during World War II. Gray's Reef Light *(below)* marks a treacherous shoal a few miles west of Waugoshance.

Nearly washed away by wind, water and ice in the early 1970s, the Round Island Lighthouse *(right)* has been restored and is a Straits area landmark.

Port Dolomite, on the east end of the Les Cheneaux Islands, is named for the brittle limestone quarried nearby. Dolomite, used to purify iron during smelting, is transported in railroad cars from the quarry *(upper right)* to Great Lakes bulk freighters at the loading dock.

(Opposite) The Straits of Mackinac has its share of abandoned islands. St. Helena was a renowned mid-nineteenth century fishing village. As the fishing industry declined in the early twentieth century, island residents moved to nearby mainland communities. Even the lightkeeper abandoned his brick-towered lighthouse when it was automated in 1923. The St. Martin's Islands *(overleaf)* are small, evergreen-covered clods in the quiet waters north of Mackinac Island.

Fifty miles north of the Straits of Mackinac, on the St. Mary's River, the twin cities of Sault Ste. Marie, Michigan *(right)* and Sault Ste. Marie, Ontario are connected by the International Bridge. Downstream from the bridge, the Sault Locks allow watercraft, from small fishing boats to 100-foot iron ore freighters, to navigate the 20-foot drop from Lake Superior to Lake Huron.

Sault Ste. Marie's hydroelectric power plant harnesses the energy of the flowing river to generate electricity for the eastern Upper Peninsula, including Mackinac Island. This 1,400-foot historic structure was built between 1896 and 1902 at a cost of $4 million.

Jesuit missionaries settled Sault Ste. Marie in 1642, making it Michigan's oldest city. Long before Europeans arrived, Chippewa Indians called this popular summer fishing spot *Bowating*, or "the rapids." Today the Sault Tribe of Chippewas has successfully used the proceeds of its casino *(center)* to develop tribal housing projects, medical facilities and businesses.

Chippewa County Airport was first constructed as Kincheloe Air Force Base in the early 1950s. Today United Express commuter planes use the runways once reserved for B-52 bombers. The old Air Force base is also home to four State of Michigan prisons including Kinross Correctional Facility, a medium-security penitentiary housing 1,200 inmates.

Pellston Regional Airport, twenty miles south of Mackinaw City, is the commercial airlink between northern lower Michigan and the rest of the world. Air passengers arriving at Pellston enjoy breathtaking views of Douglas *(left)*, Mullett and Burt Lakes, three of northern Michigan's most beautiful inland lakes.

Northern Michigan has many outstanding ski and golf resorts including Boyne Highlands near Harbor Springs. Boyne's *Heather, Moor* and *Ross* golf courses stretch along the lovely valley below the ski hills in the upper right.

(Opposite) Cheboygan is on the eastern end of the Straits of Mackinac, about 15 miles from the Mackinac Bridge. This river city is the northern port of the inland waterway which begins 40 miles away near Petoskey and flows through Crooked Lake, Burt Lake, Mullet Lake and down the Cheboygan River to the Straits of Mackinac.

Little Traverse Bay, forty miles southwest of the Straits of Mackinac, cuts deep into the northern tip of Michigan's lower peninsula. This well-protected bay is a popular playground for boating enthusiasts.

(Opposite) Harbor Springs on the bay's northern shore was first settled by Ottawa Indians who migrated south along the Lake Michigan coast from the Straits of Mackinac. By the 1880s, Harbor Springs was a popular summer resort and Harbor Point (foreground) became one of Michigan's most exclusive summer enclaves.

The city of Charlevoix was named in honor of Jesuit priest-explorer-author Father Pierre Charlevoix, who traveled through the Great Lakes in 1721 searching for a passage to the Pacific Ocean. The small village fills a spit of land that divides Lake Charlevoix from Lake Michigan *(foreground)* about 15 miles south of Petoskey.

(Opposite) Petoskey is a delightful village stretching along the southeast coast of Little Traverse Bay. This popular resort town enjoys four seasons of tourist activity from summers on the water to winters on the nearby ski hills.

Fifty miles south of Charlevoix is Traverse City, one of Michigan's most popular and fastest growing towns. Like many northern Michigan communities, Traverse City began as a booming lumber town. Today, it is the cherry capitol of the world surrounded by orchards of more than one million trees producing over half of the tart cherries consumed in the United States.

(Opposite) Mission Peninsula juts into the deep blue waters of Grand Traverse Bay. In 1839 Rev. Peter Dougherty founded a Protestant Indian mission on this 15-mile ribbon of land. Today, the verdant peninsula is home to vineyards, farmlands and some of the most attractive real estate in Michigan.

The Mackinac Bridge is a magnificent sculpture of steel, wire and concrete. Two support cables flow like giant waves over the main towers which rise more than 550 feet above the Straits. These cables, composed of thousands of individual wire strands tightly wrapped together, are anchored in giant concrete blocks which are 8,614 feet apart, making the longest single-unit suspension bridge in the world.

(Opposite) Dreams of a bridge spanning the Straits of Mackinac and connecting Michigan's two peninsulas date to the late nineteenth century. It wasn't until the early 1950s that the financial resources and human leadership combined to make the dreams reality. After three years of construction the "Mighty Mac" opened on November 1, 1957. The bridge connects Mackinaw City (foreground) with St. Ignace.

Like the birch bark trade canoes that skimmed the Straits 300 years ago, today's iron-clad, diesel-powered freighters ply these waters during the busy navigation season delivering products from around the world to Great Lakes ports.

(*Opposite*) Mackinac at sunset. The wind often drops with the sun, leaving only light ripples to catch the sun's final colors.

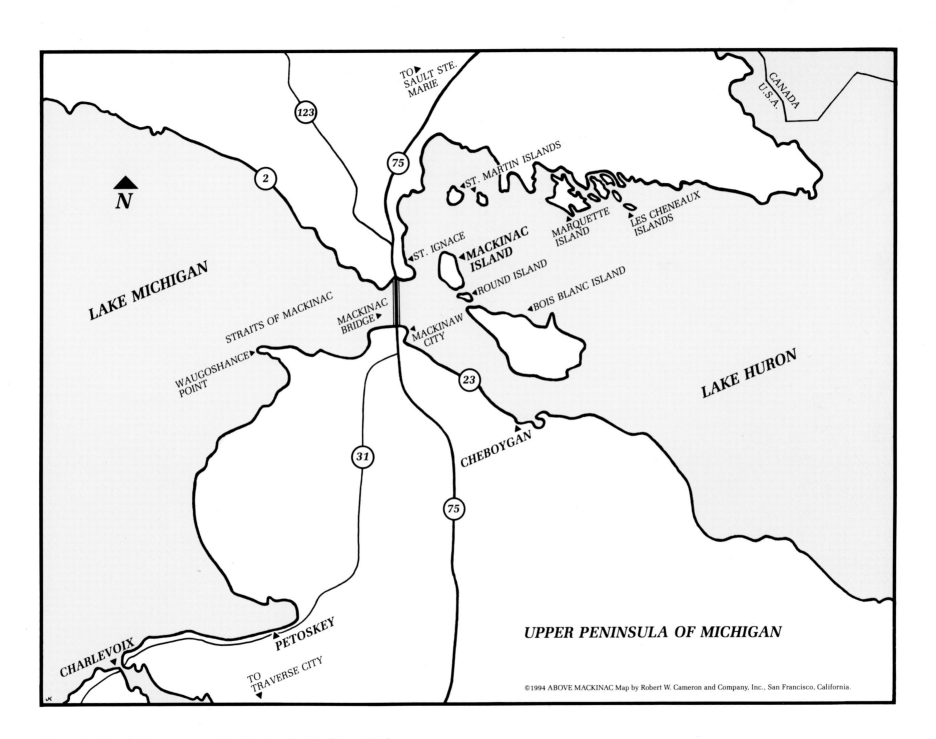

(Opposite) As darkness covers the Straits, the Mackinac Bridge fills the sky with a wave of colored lights visible for many miles.

OTHER BOOKS BY ROBERT CAMERON: *Hardcover, one hundred sixty full-color pages, 11 x 14 inches.*

ABOVE SEATTLE with Emmett Watson
ABOVE CHICAGO with Tim Samuelson and Cheryl Kent
ABOVE SAN FRANCISCO with Herb Caen
ABOVE LOS ANGELES with Jack Smith
ABOVE SAN DIEGO with Neil Morgan
ABOVE YOSEMITE with Harold Gilliam
ABOVE LONDON with Alistair Cooke
ABOVE PARIS with Pierre Salinger
ABOVE HAWAII
ABOVE WASHINGTON (D.C.)
ABOVE NEW YORK with George Plimpton and Paul Goldberger

Softcover, ninety-six full color pages, 9 x 12 inches.

ABOVE CARMEL, MONTEREY AND BIG SUR
with Harold Gilliam

Available from Cameron and Company and at fine Booksellers.